Published By Robert Corbin

@ Craig Metz

bulletproof diet: This will help you to adopt

the bulletproof diet and recalibrate your

sustainable weight loss.

All Right RESERVED

ISBN 978-87-94477-79-6

TABLE OF CONTENTS

ginger Carrot Soup 1

Cucumber Salad 3

Sweet And Salty Bulletproof Salad 5

Avocado And Salmon 7

Poached Eggs With Greens 8

Taco Salad 10

Greek Lemon Shrimp 13

Sausageburger Balls 15

Coconutcrusted Chicken 16

Chocolate Icecream (Bulletproof) 18

Chocolate Tiramisu 20

Thai Veggie Curry With Rice 22

Sweet Potato Ginger Brownies 24

'Whatever' Crockpot Dinner 26

Creamy Broccoli Soup 27

Greek Lemon Shrimp 29

Chilled Poached Salmon, Watercress Sauce, And Green Beans 31

Hake And Salmon Cakes 34

Hake Or Cod In Parchment With Salsa Verde 37

Baked Salmon 39

Ground Beef Salad 41

Easy Beef Casserole 43

Yummy Bulletproof Coffee Protein Smoothie 45

Mean Green Bulletproof Coffee Smoothie 46

Vanilla Brewed Bulletproof Coffee Smoothie 47

Delightful Sweet Potato Mess 48

Breakfast Salad 50

Roasted Lamb Rack With Cauliflower, Celery And Fennel 52

Chili 54

Meatballs 57

Beef And Mixed Vegetable Lettuce Wrap 59

Flank Steak With Fresh Greens Recipe 61

Lettuce Wrapped Grass-Fed Burger	64
Chicken Pot Pie	66
Spicy Tuna Sushi Burrito	71
Slow Cooker Beef Stew	73
Healthy Honey Mustard	76
Light & Refreshing Vinaigrette	77
Hearty Chicken Soup	78
Cauliflower And Almond Salad	80
Artichoke & Bacon Fat Salad	82
Fennel & Tangerine Side Salad	84
Sausage-Burger Balls	85
Coconut-Crusted Chicken	86
Salmon-Cuke Bites	88
Trout With Cabbage And Bacon	89
Trout Not-Fried Not-Rice	92
Braised Kalamata Beef	95
Egg N' Arugula Salad	98
Roasted Butternut	100

- Mashed Sweet Potato 102
- Frozen Chocolate Banana Monkey Bulletproof Coffee Smoothie 104
- Crunchy Almond Bulletproof Coffee Smoothie 105
- Delightful Cheesecake Bulletproof Coffee Smoothie ... 106
- Vegetable Stuffed Mushrooms 107
- Pork With Spicy Barbeque Sauce 110
- Mushroom And Meatballs In Homemade Tomato Sauce 113
- Pulled Pork With Brussels Sprouts 116
- Broccoli Soup 118
- Hanger Steak With Herb Butter 120
- Berry Bowl 122
- Cakes 123
- Bulletproof Liver Sausage 126
- Delicious Meatballs 128
- Crockpot Pork 130
- Pork Chops With Herb Crust And Wilted Dandelion Greens 132

Tres Leches Cake 134

Spinach Empanadas... 138

Avocado Stuffed With Garlic Prawns 141

Spaghetti Squash With Sage Butter And Hazelnuts 143

Sockeye Salmon Pate 145

Ginger Carrot Soup

Ingredients:

- 2 tbsp. Fresh Ginger, minced
- 1 tsp. Turmeric
- Pinch of Cinnamon
- 4 cups Vegetable stock or Bone stock
- 1 cup Unsweetened Coconut Milk (optional)
- 12 tbsp. of Grassfed butter or Ghee
- 8 Carrots, peeled and roughly chopped
- 2 Small Zucchini, peeled and roughly chopped
- 1 Small Onion, diced
- 1 Apple, peeled and roughly chopped (This is optional because it's not that bulletproof but

the flavor works well with carrots and zucchini)

- Sea salt and freshly ground black pepper

Directions:

1. Melt the butter or ghee in a saucepan on a medium heat.
2. Add the ginger and onion and cook until fragrant, this takes about 4 minutes.
3. Add the rest of vegetables, the apple, and the spices. Stir, and cook until the carrots are soft. This takes about 10 minutes.
4. Pour the stock in and bring to a boil, lower the heat and let everything simmer for 25 to 30 minutes.
5. Pour everything into a blender and puree it.
6. Pour in the coconut milk (if you are using it), season to taste, and serve warm.

Cucumber Salad

Ingredients:

- 2 tsp. of Organic Dijon mustard
- 1 pinch of Sea Salt (to taste)
- 12 Organic Cucumbers
- ¼ cup of Organic applecider vinegar
- 23 tsp. of Xylitol (or other artificial sweetener of your choice)

Directions:

1. Cut the cucumbers into thin slices.
2. Place the cucumber slices in a serving dish.
3. Generously season them with salt and allow them to sit for about 30 minutes to 1hour. (The reason behind this is to help draw the water out so you can avoid diluting the dressing. Alternatively pat them with towel.)

4. Rinse cucumber slices pat them dry.
5. Mix the Xylitol, mustard and applecider vinegar together in a large bowl.
6. Add the cucumber slices and toss well to coat them.
7. Let them sit for at least 1 hour and serve.

Sweet And Salty Bulletproof Salad

Ingredients:

- ½ lb. of Tomatoes, sliced
- 1 Small Red Onion, sliced thinly
- 2 tsp. of Brain Octane Oil (optional, Extra Virgin Olive Oil can also be used here)
- 1 Fresh Lemon
- 1 Pastured Egg, hard boiled and chopped
- ¼ lb. of Cooked Grassfed Beef, sliced
- ½ Head of Lettuce, leaves separated
- 1 Head of Radicchio, leaves separated
- Pinch of Sea Salt and Black Pepper (to taste)

Directions:

1. Create a bed of lettuce in a bowl and squeezed the juice from the lemon on the top.
2. Add the chopped egg, beef slices, tomato slices and onion slices.
3. Season the salad with pinch of sea salt and ground pepper (or cayenne) and drizzle with oil.

Avocado And Salmon

Ingredients:

- Sea salt to taste
- 8 ounces cold smoked wild sockeye salmon or 2 cold smoked wild sockeye salmon of about 4 ounces each
- 2 Hass avocadoes

Directions:

1. Peel the avocadoes. Remove the seed and discard it. Slice each of the avocadoes into 4 slices of ¼ inch thickness.
2. Place the salmon on your work area. Slice the salmon into 8 slices or each of the 4 ounces salmon into 4 slices each.
3. Place an avocado slice on one salmon slice. Sprinkle salt over it. Wrap the salmon over the avocado.

4. Serve.

Poached Eggs With Greens

Ingredients:

- 4 tablespoons grass fed butter or ghee
- ¼ cup raw cashews or almonds, sliced
- Sea salt to taste
- 6 cups collard greens or kale or Swiss chard
- 4 pastured eggs, poached

Directions:
1. Discard the hard stems and ribs of the greens you are using. Chop the greens.
2. Place a pot or saucepan over medium heat. Add water into it and bring to the boil.
3. Add greens and cook until it wilts. Drain the water.

4. Add butter and ghee to the green and mix until the butter or ghee melts and is well combined with the greens.
5. Add salt and nuts and toss well.
6. Divide into 2 plates. Place 2 eggs over each plate of greens and serve.

Taco Salad

Ingredients:

For taco mix:

- ½ pound grass fed fatty ground beef
- ½ teaspoon dried oregano
- 1 tablespoon grass fed unsalted butter or ghee
- 1 tablespoon fresh lemon juice
- ½ tablespoon cayenne powder
- Sea salt to taste

For salad:

- 1 carrot, shredded
- 4 slices avocado
- Handful of red cabbage, shredded

- ½ cup spring lettuce

- 1 small cucumber, chopped into slices

For avocado dressing:

- 2 tablespoons apple cider lemon juice

- ½ cup fresh cilantro, chopped

- Sea salt to taste

- 2 spring onions (optional)

- 1 ripe avocado, peeled, pitted, chopped

- 2 cups cucumber, sliced

- 2 tablespoons MCT oil

- 2 tablespoons fresh lemon juice

Directions:

For taco mix:

1. Place a skillet over medium heat. And beef and sauté until beef is cooked and is not pink any more.
2. Drain the fat that is in the pan.
3. Add rest of the Ingredients:and stir. Remove from heat.
4. Meanwhile, make the avocado dressing as follows: Add all the Ingredients:of the dressing into a blender and blend until smooth.
5. Mix together all the salad Ingredients:into a bowl and divide into 2 plates.
6. Divide and spoon the taco mix over it. Pour dressing over it and serve immediately.

Greek Lemon Shrimp

Ingredients:

- ½ c chopped celery
- ½ c chopped carrot
- 3 eggs
- 2 lemons (juiced)
- 1 t mct or olive oil
- 1 c chopped leeks
- 2 c shrimp

Directions:

1. In a large fry pan, cook the leeks, celery, and carrot over low heat for 510 minutes.
2. Add the shrimp (fresh or thawed) and a little water to form a broth. In a bowl, beat the eggs until frothy.

3. Continue beating the eggs as you add in the juice from the lemons and then the oil.
4. Turn off the heat under your fry pan. Remove a little hot broth from the pan and beat it into the lemon/egg mixture.
5. Pour the mixture into the fry pan and stir. Garnish with parsley and serve.

Sausageburger Balls

Ingredients:

- 1 egg
- Oregano or basil (to taste)
- ½ Lb. Spicy sausage or chorizo
- ½ lb. Ground beef

Directions:

1. Preheat oven to 325 degrees F. In a large bowl, mix all the ingredients. Form the mixture into bitesized minimeatballs.
2. Cook in a flat baking dish with sides until desired doneness is reached, about 1015 minutes.

Coconutcrusted Chicken

Ingredients:

- Fresh parsley
- Dried oregano
- 1 lb. chicken, cut into strips
- Shredded unsweetened coconut flakes or powder
- Sea salt
- 2 eggs

Directions:

1. Preheat oven to 325 degrees F. Mix the coconut, salt, parsley, and oregano in one bowl. In another bowl, beat the eggs until well blended.

2. Dip the chicken into the egg and then roll in in the dry mix until coated. Bake until it starts to brown.

Chocolate Icecream (Bulletproof)

Ingredients:

- ½ cup upgraded chocolate powder
- 50 grams of coconut oil
- 80 grams of xylitol
- 50 grams of MCT oil (this gives consistency to the icecream)
- 100 grams of water or ice
- 4 yolks of pastured eggs
- 4 full pastured eggs
- 10 drops of lemon juice
- 2 teaspoon vanilla extract
- 7 tablespoons of grassfed butter

- 50 grams cacao butter

Directions:
1. Except for water blend everything in a blender.
2. Blend it till the time all ingredient blend into creamy consistency.
3. Add water or ice and blend it for some more time till it resembles rich chocolate mousse.
4. After that pour it in icecream maker and let it do its magic.
5. Serve It The Way Your Imagination Leads You. This Comes With The Best Of Both Worlds Health And Blissful Happiness.

Chocolate Tiramisu

Ingredients:

- 2 tablespoon xylitol
- 1/3 coconut flour
- 1/3 almond meal
- ½ teaspoon sodium bicarb
- ½ teaspoon baking powder
- 50 gm grassfed butter at room temperature
- 6 separated organic eggs
- 1 tablespoon organic vanilla extract (or make your own using organic vanilla pods)
- A pinch of salt

Directions:

1. Set the oven to 170 degrees and beat xylitol, butter and yolks of eggs to a creamy texture till they are fluffy and light.
2. To this add the rest of Ingredients:except the egg whites and fold them together.
3. Now beat egg whites in a separate bowl till they form soft peaks.
4. Add 1/3 egg whites into the batter prepared and fold it carefully. Repeat the procedure till the entire mixture is used. Be carefully to retain the fluffiness.
5. Pour batter into greased tin and bake for about 30 minutes.

Thai Veggie Curry With Rice

Ingredients:

- 3 t coconut oil

- 4 leeks, sliced

- 2 cans (14 oz. each) coconut milk

- 2 zucchini, diced

- 1 sweet potato, peeled and diced

- 1 small butternut squash, peeled, seeded and diced

- 6 t thai green curry paste

- 3 limes

Directions:

1. Heat oven to 350 degrees F. Melt 2 T of the coconut oil and mix with 2 T of the

2. Thai green curry paste. Toss the sweet potato and squash in this mixture, and then put it all in a roasting pan. Season with salt and roast for about 30 minutes.
3. To begin the sauce, melt the remaining 1 T of coconut oil in a fry pan. Cook the leeks until softened and golden. Stir in the remaining 4 T of the curry paste and cook for a few minutes. Add the coconut milk and a splash of water and simmer.
4. Add the roasted vegetables along with the zucchini. Simmer for 1015 minutes.
5. Stir in the juice from the limes and serve over rice.
6. Thoroughly rinse white rice before cooking to be bulletproof. Rinse and rinse
7. until the water's clear. Then cook as usual.

Sweet Potato Ginger Brownies

Ingredients:

- 2 tsp. ground cinnamon
- ½ tsp. ground ginger
- ¼ tsp. vanilla powder
- ¼ tsp. baking powder
- pinch sea salt
- 2 c cooked mashed sweet potato (purple ones if you can get them)
- 3 eggs
- ¼ c butter
- ¼ c raw honey
- 3 T coconut flour

- 3 T dark cocoa powder

- ½ c chopped Lindt 90% dark chocolate bar

Directions:

1. Preheat oven to 350 degrees F. Mix the mashed sweet potato with the eggs, butter, honey, and vanilla. Combine well.
2. Add in the coconut flour, cocoa powder, spices, baking powder, and salt. Again mix well. Stir in the chocolate pieces.
3. Spread the batter in a buttered 8x8 pan. Bake 35-45 minutes until a toothpick comes out fairly clean. Cool before cutting.

'Whatever' Crockpot Dinner

Ingredients:

- 12 'green zone' vegetables, chopped
- Spinach or kale
- 1 'green zone' meat
- Your choice herbs/spices

Directions:

1. Put some coconut oil in a pan on medium heat. Lightly brown the meat and then add the veggies and your leafy greens. Sprinkle in your spices and herbs.
2. Stir, cover, and cook on low for 68 hours.

Creamy Broccoli Soup

Ingredients:

- 4 c bone broth or veggie broth
- ½ c grass-fed butter
- Sea salt to taste
- 6-8 cups broccoli florets
- 3-4 shallots, minced
- 1 carrot, sliced

Directions:
1. Put a dab of butter into a large stockpot and lightly sauté the shallots and carrot. Add the broccoli and cook until it's bright green.
2. Pour in the broth and continue to cook until broccoli is tender.

3. Add the remaining butter and blend (a hand blender works well) until desired consistency. Season with sea salt and serve hot.

Greek Lemon Shrimp

Ingredients:

- 3 eggs
- 2 lemons (juiced)
- 1 T MCT or olive oil
- 2 c shrimp
- 1 c chopped leeks
- ½ c chopped celery
- ½ c chopped carrot

Directions:

1. In a large fry pan, cook the leeks, celery, and carrot over low heat for 5-10 minutes.
2. Add the shrimp (fresh or thawed) and a little water to form a broth. In a bowl, beat the eggs until frothy.

3. Continue beating the eggs as you add in the juice from the lemons and then the oil. Turn off the heat under your fry pan.
4. Remove a little hot broth from the pan and beat it into the lemon/egg mixture. Pour the mixture into the fry pan and stir. Garnish with parsley and serve.

Chilled Poached Salmon, Watercress Sauce, And Green Beans

Ingredients:

- 1/3 cup packed fresh basil leaves
- 1/2 cup Bulletproof Mayonnaise 2 1/2 teaspoons fresh lemon juice
- Sea salt
- 8 ounces green beans
- 2 skinless wild salmon fillets (8 ounces each)
- 1 tablespoon grass-fed unsalted butter
- 1 bunch watercress
- 1 tablespoon Bulletproof Brain Octane oil (or MCT or coconut oil)

Directions:

1. In a medium saucepan, combine the salmon and butter and add enough water to just cover the salmon.
2. Cover the pan, bring to a simmer over medium heat, and simmer until the salmon is just cooked through, about 12 minutes total. Use a fish spatula or slotted spoon to transfer the salmon to a plate.
3. Drain the saucepan and set aside to use again. Refrigerate the salmon until chilled, about 1 hour.
4. Have a large bowl of ice water ready. Add 1/4 cup tap water to the reserved saucepan.
5. Cover and bring to a simmer over medium heat. Add the watercress, cover, and cook until wilted, about 1 minute.
6. Transfer the watercress to the ice water to stop the cooking. Squeeze out excess water and coarsely chop.

7. In a blender, combine the watercress, basil, and mayonnaise and process until smooth. Add 1 teaspoon of the lemon juice and season with salt to taste.
8. Add 1 cup of water to the saucepan, cover, and bring to a simmer over medium heat.
9. Add the green beans, cover, and cook until just tender, 2 to 3 minutes. Drain the beans and toss with the Brain Octane oil, remaining 1 1/2 teaspoons lemon juice, and salt to taste.
10. Serve the salmon with the watercress sauce and green beans.

Hake And Salmon Cakes

Ingredients:

- 2 tablespoons olive oil

- 1 tablespoon Bulletproof Brain Octane oil (or MCT or coconut oil) 1/2 pound skinless wild sockeye salmon, cut into 1/4-inch cubes

- 1/2 pound skinless hake, cut into 1/4-inch cubes

- 1/4 cup finely chopped fresh flat-leaf parsley

- 1/4 cup sweet rice flour

- 1 large pastured egg

- 1 tablespoon fresh lemon juice

- 1 tablespoon Dijon mustard

- Sea salt

- 2 teaspoons ghee

Directions:

1. Line a plate with parchment paper and set aside.
2. In a food processor, pulse together the egg, lemon juice, mustard, and a
3. pinch of sea salt. As it pulses, drizzle the oils slowly into the food processor to combine.
4. Add half of the salmon and hake and pulse to a coarse paste. Fold in the remaining fish and parsley, then fold in the sweet rice flour.
5. With wet hands, to prevent sticking, divide the mixture into 4 patties 3 inches wide and 3/4 inch thick.
6. Place the cakes on the plate and refrigerate until chilled and firm, about 1 hour.
7. Preheat the oven to 320°F.
8. In a large ovenproof skillet, melt the ghee over medium heat. Add the fish cakes to the

pan and cook, turning once, until firm on the outside, about 8 minutes.

9. Transfer the pan to the oven and bake until the cakes are hot, about 10 minutes.

Hake Or Cod In Parchment With Salsa Verde

Ingredients:

- 1 tablespoon grass-fed unsalted butter, cut into small pieces 2 lemon slices (1/4 inch thick)

- 1 fennel bulb (10 ounces), trimmed, cored, and thinly sliced

- 2 hake or cod fillets (1/2 pound each) Sea salt

- Salsa Verde

Directions:
1. Preheat the oven to 320°F. Line a baking dish with parchment paper. Place the fillets on the parchment paper, season with salt, and dot with the butter.
2. Place a lemon slice on each fillet. Wrap the parchment around the fillets, folding seams, and tucking in the sides so no steam escapes.

3. Bake until the fish is just cooked through, 20 to 25 minutes, depending on thickness.
4. Toss the fennel with 2 tablespoons of the salsa verde. Serve the fennel and remaining salsa with the fillets.

Baked Salmon

Ingredients:

- 3 tablespoons capers
- ½ teaspoon paprika
- ¼ cup olive oil
- 1 red onion, chopped
- 250g salmon cut into fillets
- 1 cup kalamata olives
- 1 tomato, chopped
- 1 Tablespoon fresh lemon juice
- Pinch of salt, pinch of pepper

Directions:

1. Season fish fillets with paprika, pinch of salt and pepper and then set aside.

2. In a bowl, combine onion, capers, lemon juice, tomato, olives, pinch of salt and pepper. Pour the mixture over the fish fillets and then wrap them in an aluminum foil; make sure to seal the edges of the aluminum foil.
3. Bake the wrapped fish fillets in the oven at 350 °F for about 30 minutes or until cooked through.

Ground Beef Salad

Ingredients:

- 2 cups spring greens

- 1 cucumber, sliced thinly

- 2 avocados, peeled and pitted ¼ cup apple cider vinegar

- ¼ cup freshly-squeezed lemon juice ¼ cup coconut oil, melted

- ½ cup cilantro, chopped

- 250 grams ground beef

- 1 tablespoon cayenne pepper

- 3 tablespoons fresh-squeezed lime water

- 2 tablespoons butter

- 1/2 cup chopped red cabbage

- Pinch of salt

Directions:

1. Sauté the ground beef in a nonstick pan. Cook beef for about 5 minutes or until cooked through.
2. Add the butter, cayenne pepper and lime juice to the beef. Season the beef mixture with salt and then set aside. Meanwhile, put the avocados, vinegar, lemon juice, cilantro and coconut oil in the blender; blend until the mixture is smooth and then set it aside.
3. Put all the vegetables and the beef in a large salad bowl. Pour the avocado dressing over the salad and then toss to combine.

Easy Beef Casserole

Ingredients:

- 2 large turnips
- 3 scallions, chopped
- 4 eggs, beaten
- 250 grams ground pork
- 2 tablespoons coconut oil
- Pinch of salt

Directions:
1. Rinse turnips and pat dry. Peel them, grate them and then set aside.
2. Heat coconut oil in a pan and then cook meat until cooked through. Set aside to cool.

3. Add the scallions, turnips and eggs to the cooled meat. Season with a pinch of salt and then mix well.
4. Transfer the mixture on a baking pan and bake at 400 °F for about 40 minutes.
5. Cover the baking pan with aluminum foil and bake for another 20 minutes.
6. Let the casserole cool before serving.

Yummy Bulletproof Coffee Protein Smoothie

Ingredients:

- 1 tablespoon of cocoa powder, unsweetened
- 1 scoop of chocolate protein powder, or of choice
- 1 cup of brewed Bulletproof Coffee, chilled
- 1 cup of ice
- 1 cup of almond milk, or of choice
- 1 chopped organic banana, frozen
- 1 tablespoon of raw honey

Directions:
1. Gather all of the listed Ingredients:, add them into a blender and blend until the mixture is smooth.

Mean Green Bulletproof Coffee Smoothie

Ingredients:

- ½ cup of fresh spinach
- 1 cup of ice, or less
- 1 tablespoon of raw honey
- ½ tablespoon of coco powder, unsweetened
- 4 tablespoons of Bulletproof Coffee, chilled
- 1 cup of almond milk, or of choice
- 1 chopped organic banana, frozen

Directions:
1. Combine all of the listed Ingredients: into a blender and blend until the mixture is even and smooth.

Vanilla Brewed Bulletproof Coffee Smoothie

Ingredients:

- ½ cup of vanilla protein powder, or of choice
- ½ cup of raw organic heavy cream
- 2 cups of ice, or less
- 1 cup of brewed Bulletproof Coffee, chilled
- ¼ cup of raw organic yogurt, or of choice

Directions:

1. Combine all of the listed Ingredients: into a blender and blend the mixture until it is smooth.

Delightful Sweet Potato Mess

Ingredients:

- 2 teaspoons organic flat-leaf parsley, finely chopped
- 2 pastured pork sausage links
- Generous pat of extra virgin olive oil
- 1 pastured egg (optional)
- 1 organically grown spring onion, finely chopped
- 2 organically grown chopped sweet potatoes, peeled and cut into small cubes
- Sea salt and pepper as per taste

Directions:

1. Heat a grilling pan and cook the sausages over it till they are cooked all the way through and

are nice brown in color. This should take 20-25 minutes and be careful to do it at low flame.
2. Take them off and on the same grill drizzle some olive oil and spring onion.
3. Once the onions are also grilled put the sausages and onions in a large pot with salt to taste, stirring occasionally.
4. Then all the cubed sweet potatoes go into the pot. Once it begins to get pulpy close the lid for about 10-12 minutes let it cook in its own juices, stirring in between.
5. Finally toss in chopped parsley and let the aroma infuse the dish.
6. This is a complete meal in itself, but if you need you could team it with any variety of egg making it more filling and wholesome.

Breakfast Salad

Ingredients:

- 1 avocado, organic
- 1 broccoli, organic
- 2 pastured eggs
- Generous pat of grass-fed butted or extra virgin coconut oil
- A big bunch of organically grown tender and fresh spinach
- 1 carrot, organic
- 1 celery stick, organic
- Sea salt (optional)

Directions:

1. Peel or scrape the carrot and cut it into small pieces.
2. Chop the celery stalk.
3. Scrape the pulpy and fleshy part of avocado and cut it into small pieces.
4. Cut broccoli and boil it for 5-7 minutes.
5. Chop spinach and boil it for 2-3 minutes.
6. Once these two cool, all the vegetable go into a big mixing bowl.
7. You could also use some more vegetables of your choice, but make sure to cook the ones that need to be cooked like it is done with spinach and broccoli.
8. Now take the eggs and cook the way you like them best. They can be boiled, poached, or fried in grass fed butter.
9. Once the eggs are also done toss them into the bowl along with vegetable. Dash it with salt and freshly ground black pepper.

Roasted Lamb Rack With Cauliflower, Celery And Fennel

Ingredients:

- 4 cups fennel, sliced
- 4 cups cauliflower, sliced
- 4 cups celery, sliced
- Sea salt to taste
- 2 tablespoons each of fresh thyme, oregano, rosemary and sage, chopped
- 2 American rack of grass fed organic lamb chops (8 chops each) (about 3 pounds)
- 2 tablespoons ghee, melted
- 2 tablespoons fresh turmeric, chopped

Directions:

1. Apply ghee over the lamb and rub well. Cut lines on the top diagonally.
2. Sprinkle salt, turmeric, and all the herbs over the lamb.
3. Place the vegetables in a large baking dish. Place the lamb over it with the fat side facing up.
4. Bake in a preheated oven at 350 F for about 45 minutes or until the internal temperature in the thickest part of the lamb shows 125 F.
5. When done, broil for 3 minutes or until crisp.

Chili

Ingredients:

- 3 tablespoons ancho chili powder
- 1 ½ teaspoons cayenne chili powder
- Sea salt to taste
- Pepper to taste
- 3 tablespoons ground cumin
- ½ teaspoon ground cinnamon
- 3 tablespoons fresh oregano
- 3 teaspoons gluten free beer
- ¾ ounce bulletproof chocolate bar, grated
- 1 ½ cups onions, chopped
- 2 teaspoons grass fed butter

- 1 ½ tablespoons upgraded XTC oil

- 2 ¼ pounds grass fed ground beef

- 8 cloves garlic, chopped

- 9 medium tomatoes, chopped

- 1 ½ teaspoons chipotle chili powder

- 1/3 cup organic tomato paste

- 1 ½ butternut squash, cubed

- 2 cups water

- ¾ cup organic chicken broth

Directions:

1. Place butternut squash on a baking sheet. Add XCT oil and toss. Bake at 350 F until tender.
2. Place a skillet over medium heat. Add butter. When the butter melts, add most of the garlic

cloves and 1-cup onions and sauté until translucent.
3. Add beef and sauté until brown, breaking it simultaneously as it cooks.
4. Add spices, stir and remove from heat.
5. Add tomatoes, a little salt, water, remaining onion, and garlic to a pot and place the pot over medium heat. Simmer for 5-6 minutes.
6. Lower heat, add basil and oregano and continue simmering for a couple of minutes. Add rest of the Ingredients: and simmer for 10 minutes.
7. Add baked butternut squash, stir and serve.

Meatballs

Ingredients:

For the meatballs:

- ¼ teaspoon ground black pepper or to taste
- 1 ½ teaspoons turmeric powder
- 1 ½ tablespoons grass fed butter
- 2 small pastured eggs
- 1 ½ pound grass fed organic ground lamb
- 1/3 cup almonds, ground
- ¼ cup fresh parsley leaves, minced
- ½ tablespoon paprika
- 1 teaspoon ground cumin
- ½ teaspoon salt

Directions:

1. To make the meatballs: Mix together all the Ingredients: of the meatballs using your hands. Mix until well combined.
2. Using your hands, make small meatballs of about 1 inch diameter and place them on a baking sheet. Bake in a preheated oven at 320 F for about 25 minutes.
3. Serve hot as it is or with gravy of your choice.

Beef And Mixed Vegetable Lettuce Wrap

Ingredients:

- 1 zucchini
- ½ lb. Of grass-fed ground beef
- Sea salt (to taste)
- 2 tsp. Of extra virgin olive oil
- 1 iceberg lettuce
- 4-5 tsp. Of chinese cooking-alcohol
- 4 to 5 cloves of garlic
- 2-3 carrots
- 1 large cucumber
- 1 squash
- 1 green onion

Directions:

1. Dice the vegetables and chop the green onions and garlic.
2. Heat 2 tsp. of olive oil in a pot over medium-low heat and then add the ground beef. Stir slowly until it's completely cooked. Take the beef out of the pot and set it aside.
3. Put the chopped garlic and green onion in the pot and then add the carrots. Stir well and cook for about 3 to 4 minutes.
4. Add 4 to 5 tsp. of Chinese cooking-alcohol to help bring the flavor out.
5. Add the remaining vegetables and salt to taste. Add ½ cup water if needed and cook for about 4-5 minutes.
6. Add the beef back to pot and cook everything for about 1-2 more minutes until all the vegetables are cooked.
7. Wrap everything in lettuce and serve.

Flank Steak With Fresh Greens Recipe

Ingredients:

For main dish:

- 8 Cherry Tomatoes, halved

- 2 Green Onions, thinly sliced

- 2 tbsp. Grass-fed Butter

- Sea Salt and Freshly Ground Black Pepper

- 8 oz. Grass-fed Beef flank steak

- 2 cups Mixed Greens

- 1 Sweet Bell Pepper, chopped

For dressing:

- ½ tsp. Chili Powder

- ¼ tsp. Ground cumin

- Sea Salt (to taste)

- 2 tbsp. Shallots, minced

- 3 tbsp. Fresh Lime Juice

- 1 tbsp. Extra Virgin Olive Oil

- 1 Clove of Garlic, minced

Directions:

1. Prepare the dressing by mixing all the Ingredients: together in a bowl.
2. Season the steak before cooking with some sea salt and freshly ground black pepper.
3. Melt the grass-fed butter (you can use some animal fat here instead) in a skillet placed over a medium heat.
4. Cook the steak for 4 to 5 minutes per side for a medium-rare cook. Then cut the steak into thin slices.

5. Put the steak on a plate along with the mixed greens, drizzle with the dressing and serve.

Lettuce Wrapped Grass-Fed Burger

Ingredients:

- Iceberg lettuce

- 2 Avocados

- 4-5 Garlic Cloves,

- ½ Tomato

- ½ lb. of Grass-fed ground beef

- Sea Salt (to taste)

Directions:
1. Shape the ground beef into patties with beef and grill them until they are ready.
2. Meanwhile, dice the tomato, avocados and garlic.
3. Mix them in a bowl and add the salt to taste. This will make a kind of salsa.

4. Use the lettuce in place of a traditional burger bap, add the meat and vegetables and serve.

Chicken Pot Pie

Ingredients:

Pie crust

- ½ tsp salt
- ½ tsp baking powder
- 3 eggs (divided, reserve 1 for egg wash)
- 1 tsp water
- 1/3 cup Bulletproof Grass-Fed Ghee
- 2¾ cup blanched almond flour
- 3 tbsp coconut flour
- 1 tsp xanthan gum

Filling

- ½ cup green beans (chopped into small pieces)

- 1 tsp garlic (minced)
- ¼ tsp xanthan gum
- 2½ cups chicken thighs (cooked; chopped or shredded)
- 1½ scoops Bulletproof Collagelatin
- 2 tbsp Bulletproof Grass-Fed Ghee
- Fresh thyme sprigs (for garnish)
- 2 celery stalks (chopped)
- 1 medium onion (chopped)
- 1½ tsp fresh thyme (chopped)
- ½ tsp salt
- ½ tsp pepper
- 1½ cups chicken broth

Directions:

1. Preheat oven to 350°F.
2. In a mixing bowl, whisk together the almond flour, coconut flour, xanthan gum, salt and baking powder. Add the Ghee and 2 eggs (reserve the third egg for the egg wash). Mix to form a dough. Shape it into a disk and divide in half.
3. Wrap or cover each half and chill in the freezer for 15-20 minutes.
4. Warm a large skillet over medium heat. Add 2 tablespoons of Ghee.
5. Add the celery, onion and thyme to the skillet and cook for 10-15 minutes, or until the vegetables have softened. Add the salt and pepper.
6. Add the chicken broth, green beans and garlic. Bring the mixture to a boil, then reduce and simmer for 10 minutes.
7. Whisk in the Collagelatin and xanthan gum. Remove from heat.

8. Fold in the chicken. Let the mixture cool.
9. Place one of the chilled dough balls on a piece of parchment paper on a flat surface. Use a rolling pin to roll it out about 1/4-inch thick. Carefully pick up the sheet of parchment with the dough and place it into the pie dish. Peel away the parchment. Fit the dough into the dish, shaping the pie crust and crimping the edges (optional).
10. Use a fork to poke holes into the bottom of the crust. Par-bake the crust for 10-12 minutes. While it bakes, roll out the second half to 1/4-inch thickness.
11. Remove from the oven and pour the cooled filling into the crust. Gently place the remaining dough over the pie filling, pressing the edges together to seal. Cut three slits in the top.

12. Whisk together the egg wash Ingredients: (the remaining egg and water), Brush the egg wash onto the pot pie crust.
13. Transfer the pie to the oven and bake at 350°F for 25-27 minutes, or until the crust is golden-brown. Remove and let it rest for 10 minutes.
14. To serve, cut 8 pie slices. Plate, fork and enjoy!
15. Store leftovers in an air-tight container in the refrigerator for up to 5 days.

Spicy Tuna Sushi Burrito

Ingredients:

- ¼ avocado
- 1 cucumber (julienned/thinly sliced)
- 2 tsp green onions
- 1 tsp sesame seeds
- 1 tbsp Bulletproof-friendly mayonnaise
- 1 tsp sriracha
- ½ cup raw tuna (cubed; sub salmon if concerned about mercury)
- ¾ cup cauliflower rice (cooked and chilled down to room temperature)
- 1 tsp Bulletproof Brain Octane C8 MCT Oil
- 1 nori (seaweed) sheets

Directions:

1. Cook and then cool cauliflower rice in a bowl. Mix with MCT Oil.
2. Slice avocado and cucumber. Chop scallions and set aside.
3. Slice uncooked tuna into even-sized cubes.
4. Mix cubed tuna with mayo and sriracha in a small bowl until evenly coated.
5. Place sheet or nori on sushi mat.
6. Spread cauliflower rice thoroughly on nori, leaving a small empty spot at the top.
7. Add the filling (tuna mixture, avocado and cucumber) in small strains in the direction of the middle of the nori. Top with green onions and sprinkle with sesame seeds.
8. Moisten the top of the nori sheet with a bit of water before you roll your burrito.
9. Slice in half and enjoy the fresh, vibrant flavors of this keto-pleasant sushi burrito!

Slow Cooker Beef Stew

Ingredients:

- 1 tablespoon chopped ginger

- 3 garlic cloves, minced (optional)

- 1 leek, white part only with the hard outer layer removed

- One 15-ounce can diced tomatoes (BPA-free)

- 3 handfuls fresh spinach

- 2 tablespoons apple cider vinegar

- 2 teaspoons dried rosemary, or 1 sprig (leaves only)

- 2 teaspoons dried thyme or 2 sprigs (leaves only)

- 2 teaspoons dried oregano

- 3 - 3 1/2 pounds grass-fed beef, diced

- 1 1/2 cups beef bone broth

- 3 stalks of celery, chopped

- 3 carrots, chopped into large rounds

- 1 tablespoon Grass-Fed Ghee or coconut oil

- Salt and pepper to taste

Directions:

1. In a frying pan on medium heat, add ghee and gently brown beef (you might also additionally have to work in batches). Add beef to your slow cooker.
2. Add all remaining ingredients besides spinach to your sluggish cooker and stir to combine well.
3. Turn the heat to low, and cook for 5-eight hours.
4. Before cooking time finishes, gently steam spinach and set aside.
5. Once cooking time is complete, gently stir in spinach.
6. Taste the mix and add more flavoring if desired (such as more dried herbs, sparkling lemon juice, or tomato paste).
7. Serve slow cooker beef stew warm with mashed cauliflower, steamed greens, or cooked and cooled white rice.

Healthy Honey Mustard

Ingredients:

- ¼ cup apple cider vinegar
- 1/8 cup extra virgin olive oil
- 1/8 cup MCT oil
- 1 tablespoon mustard
- 2 tablespoons honey, raw

Directions:
1. Blend all Ingredients: until smooth. Serve with a bulletproof salad.

Light & Refreshing Vinaigrette

Ingredients:

- ½ avocado
- ¼ cup extra virgin olive oil
- 2 tablespoons MCT oil
- ¼ cup apple cider vinegar
- Handful fresh basil, finely chopped

Directions:

1. Blend all Ingredients: in food processor until smooth. Pour over your favorite Bulletproof salad.

Hearty Chicken Soup

Ingredients:

- 1 cup cauliflower, chopped
- 8 cups water, filtered
- 1 inch fresh ginger, peeled and finely chopped
- Sea salt, to taste
- 1 cup celery, finely chopped
- 1 cup broccoli, chopped
- 1 cup spinach, finely chopped
- 1 pound ground chicken, grass-fed and organic

Directions:

1. In a large pot, boil vegetables, water, ginger, and sea salt. If desired, incorporate additional seasonings, such as thyme or oregano.
2. When water is boiling, add chicken directly to the mixture.
3. Once the chicken is thoroughly cooked and the vegetables are tender, remove from heat and serve.

Cauliflower And Almond Salad

Ingredients:

- 3 tablespoons apple cider vinegar
- 3 tablespoons honey
- 4 tablespoon coconut oil
- ¼ teaspoon turmeric
- ¼ cup cilantro, finely chopped
- 3 cups cauliflower, finely sliced
- 2 cups red lettuce, finely sliced
- ¼ cup flaked almonds
- Salt and pepper to taste

Directions:

1. Combine the vinegar, honey coconut oil and salt & pepper into a small bowl and mix well.

2. In a large salad bowl add the remaining Ingredients: and mix.
3. Pour over the dressing and serve!

Artichoke & Bacon Fat Salad

Ingredients:

- ¼ cup chives, chopped
- ¼ cup warm bacon fat
- 3 tablespoon apple cider vinegar
- 1 tablespoon honey
- 2 cups artichoke in oil
- 1 head of cos lettuce, finely sliced
- 5 radish, sliced
- Salt and pepper to taste

Directions:

1. Warm the bacon fat in a small sauce pan and add the honey, vinegar and chives.

2. Combine the artichoke, radish and lettuce in a bowl.
3. Pour over the dressing and mix well.
4. Serve immediately.

Fennel & Tangerine Side Salad

Ingredients:

- Juice of 1 lemon
- 3 tablespoon virgin olive oil
- Salt and pepper to taste
- 2 fennel bulbs, finely sliced
- 1 tangerine, segmented
- ¼ cup flat leaf parsley, chopped

Directions:
1. Combine all the Ingredients: together in a bowl.
2. Serve immediately.

Sausage-Burger Balls

Ingredients:

- ½ lb. spicy sausage or chorizo
- ½ lb. ground beef
- 1 egg
- oregano or basil (to taste)

Directions:

1. Preheat oven to 325 degrees F. In a large bowl, mix all the ingredients.
2. Form the mixture into bite-sized mini-meatballs.
3. Cook in a flat baking dish with sides until desired doneness is reached, about 10-15 minutes.

Coconut-Crusted Chicken

Ingredients:

- Fresh parsley
- Dried oregano
- 1 lb. chicken, cut into strips
- 2 eggs
- Shredded unsweetened coconut flakes or powder
- Sea salt

Directions:

1. Preheat oven to 325 degrees F. Mix the coconut, salt, parsley, and oregano in one bowl.
2. In another bowl, beat the eggs until well blended.

3. Dip the chicken into theegg and then roll in in the dry mix until coated. Bake until it starts to brown.

Salmon-Cuke Bites

Ingredients:

- Cucumber, cut into ½ inch pieces

- Sea salt

- Smoked salmon

Directions:

1. Cut the salmon into strips, and wrap each strip around a piece of cucumber (or zucchini or avocado). Season with salt or salad dressing (as desired).

Trout With Cabbage And Bacon

Ingredients:

- 3 tablespoons grass-fed unsalted butter, cut into small pieces 1 tablespoon apple cider vinegar

- Coarse sea salt

- 2 wild trout (8 to 9 ounces each), cleaned and butterflied by fishmonger 1/2 scallion, diced (optional)

- 6 lemon slices (1/8 inch thick), plus juice to taste for serving

- 2 thick-cut slices pastured slab bacon (3 ounces total), cut into 1/4-inch lardons 6 cups 1/2-inch-thick strips savoy cabbage

- 2 sprigs fresh thyme plus 2 teaspoons thyme leaves

- 1/4 cup water

- 2 teaspoons Bulletproof Brain Octane oil (or MCT or coconut oil)

Directions:

1. Preheat the oven to 320°F.
2. In a large, high-sided ovenproof skillet with a lid, cook the bacon over medium-low heat, stirring occasionally, until cooked but not browned, about 5 minutes.
3. Add the cabbage, thyme sprigs, and water. Cover and cook, stirring occasionally, until tender, 8 to 10 minutes.
4. Stir in 1 tablespoon of the butter and the vinegar. Remove the thyme and season with salt to taste.
5. Transfer the cabbage and bacon to a bowl and set aside in a warm place. Wipe out and reserve the skillet.

6. Place both fish, open, on a cutting board. Top each with 1 tablespoon butter, 1 teaspoon thyme leaves, diced scallion (if using), and salt to taste. Place 3 lemon slices into each fish and close the trout.
7. Rub the fish with the Brain Octane oil, transfer to the reserved skillet, cover, and bake until just firm and opaque, 18 to 20 minutes. Season to taste with lemon juice and salt.

Trout Not-Fried Not-Rice

Ingredients:

- 3/4 teaspoon ground coriander

- 1/2 cup grated carrots (about 2 small carrots)

- 1 celery stalk, cut into 1/8-inch-thick slices (about 1/2 cup)

- 3 tablespoons water

- 2 1/2 ounces smoked trout, flaked

- 1 cauliflower, cut into 2-inch florets 2 large pastured eggs

- Sea salt, to taste

- 1 tablespoon ghee

- 1 tablespoon Bulletproof Brain Octane oil (or MCT or coconut oil)

- 1 scallion, thinly sliced, white and dark green parts kept separate

- 1 tablespoon minced peeled fresh ginger

- 1/2 teaspoon fresh lime juice

Directions:

1. In a food processor, pulse the cauliflower until evenly broken into small grains, working in batches as necessary.
2. In a small bowl, lightly beat the eggs with salt.
3. In a large skillet, heat the ghee over medium heat. Add the eggs and swirl to coat the pan.
4. Reduce the heat to medium-low and cook until the eggs are just set, 1 to 2 minutes.
5. Remove the eggs to a plate and slice into thin strips.
6. Wipe out the pan, return to medium heat, and add the Brrain Octane oil, scallion whites, and ginger.

7. Cook until fragrant, about 30 seconds. Add the coriander, carrots, celery, cauliflower, and water.
8. Cook, stirring constantly, until the vegetables are crisp-tender, about 6 minutes. Stir in the smoked trout, lime juice, egg strips, and scallion greens. Season with salt to taste.

Braised Kalamata Beef

Ingredients:

- 1 carrot, coarsely chopped
- 1/2 cup water
- 1 teaspoon apple cider vinegar
- 1 tablespoon dried oregano
- 1 bay leaf
- 1 teaspoon coarse sea salt
- 1 tablespoon chopped parsley leaves
- 1/2 cup ghee or grass-fed unsalted butter
- 1 tablespoon Bulletproof Brain Octane oil
- 1 tablespoon sesame oil

- 1 bunch scallions, white and light green parts only, thinly sliced

- 1 bunch broccoli, stems peeled and finely chopped, florets cut into 1-inch pieces 1 piece (2 inches) fresh ginger, peeled and thinly sliced

- 1 orange

- 1 pound boneless grass-fed sirloin, thinly sliced

- 1/2 cup Kalamata olives, pitted

Directions:

1. In a Dutch oven or large pot, combine the white parts of the scallions, broccoli stems, and ginger and cook over low heat until fragrant, about 5 minutes.
2. Meanwhile, grate 1 teaspoon of zest from the orange (set the zest aside). Then peel and segment the orange (see How to Segment Citrus).
3. Add the broccoli florets, orange segments, beef, olives, carrot, water, vinegar, oregano, bay leaf, and salt to the pot.
4. Cover and cook until the beef is tender and the vegetables are crisp tender, at least 10 minutes.
5. Stir in the green parts of the scallions, the orange zest, parsley, ghee, Brain Octane oil, and sesame oil.

Egg N' Arugula Salad

Ingredients:

- 2 eggs
- ½ cup coconut oil
- 1 tablespoon freshly-squeezed lemon juice
- 1 tablespoon apple cider vinegar
- Pinch of salt
- 2 cups arugula
- 1 avocado, peeled, pitted and sliced thinly
- 2 radishes, sliced thinly
- Pinch of pepper

Directions:

1. Put arugula, avocado and the radish slices on a large salad bowl.

2. Add the coconut oil, lemon juice and a pinch of salt and pepper to the bowl and then toss all the Ingredients: to combine.
3. Fill a pan with water, add the vinegar to the water and bring the mixture to a boil.
4. Remove the pan from heat. Crack each egg into a ramekin and then gently slide them into the water, one at a time. Cover the pan and let the eggs set for about 5 minutes.
5. Remove the eggs from the pan and let them drain. Put the eggs on top of the salad and then serve immediately.

Roasted Butternut

Ingredients:

- 2 cloves garlic, minced
- Pinch of salt
- Pinch of pepper
- 1 butternut squash
- 1 tablespoon coconut oil
- 1 tablespoon unsalted butter, melted

Directions:
1. Peel the butternut squash and remove the seeds. Cut it into bitesize cubes.
2. Put the cubes in a bowl and toss with coconut oil and butter.

3. Season them with salt and pepper and then arrange them in a baking sheet in a single layer.
4. Put the baking sheet in the oven and roast the butternut squash at 400 °F for about 30 minutes or until lightly browned.

Mashed Sweet Potato

Ingredients:

- 3 tablespoons butter
- 2 tablespoons sweetener
- Pinch of salt
- 3 sweet potatoes
- ½ cup milk
- Pinch puff pepper

Directions:

1. Rinse the sweet potatoes and then place them in a pot.
2. Cover them with water and then bring it to a boil. Cook the sweet potatoes for about 10 to 15 minutes or until tender.

3. Remove the sweet potatoes from the pot and let them cool.
4. Peel the sweet potatoes and mash them using a fork. Set the mashed sweet potato aside.
5. In a saucepan, mix milk, sweetener and butter and then let it simmer for about 3 minutes.
6. Pour the mixture over the mashed sweet potatoes and mix well.
7. Season the mashed sweet potatoes with a pinch of salt and pepper.

Frozen Chocolate Banana Monkey Bulletproof Coffee Smoothie

Ingredients:

- 1 ½ cups of almond milk, or coconut
- 2 teaspoons of raw cacao powder, or of choice
- 2 organic pitted dates
- 2 sliced organic bananas, frozen
- 4 shots of Bulletproof coffee, chilled
- 1 tablespoon of ground chia seeds (Optional)

Directions:

1. Combine all of the Ingredients: into a blender and blend until the mixture is smooth.

Crunchy Almond Bulletproof Coffee Smoothie

Ingredients:

- 4 oz. of almond milk, or coconut
- 1 sliced organic banana, frozen
- 2 tbsp. of whole almonds
- 4 oz. of Bulletproof Coffee, chilled
- 2 tsp. of natural cocoa powder

Directions:

1. Combine all of the Ingredients: into a blender and blend until the mixture is even and smooth.

Delightful Cheesecake Bulletproof Coffee Smoothie

Ingredients:

- 3 teaspoons of raw honey
- 1 med. frozen organic banana, chilled
- 1 cup of ice
- ½ cup of almond milk, or coconut
- ¼ cup of Cottage Cheese, or of choice
- 1 tablespoon of Cocoa powder, unsweetened
- 1 small teaspoon of instant Bulletproof Coffee,

Directions:

1. Add all of the Ingredients: into a blender and blend the mixture until it is smooth.

Vegetable Stuffed Mushrooms

Ingredients:

- 1 Capsicum
- Diced mushroom stem
- 1 chopped onion
- 1 tsp chili flakes
- 1 tsp black pepper
- 8 cloves of minced garlic
- 1 egg (enriched with Omega 3)
- 8 large fresh organic button mushrooms
- pounds minced beef (Grass-fed; essential for a Bulletproof Diet)
- Diced celery stalks

- ¼ cup olive oil

- ¼ cup fine coconut flour

Directions:

1. Clean the mushroom and cut off their stem, scooping off their dark feathery insides. Make sure they are dry before cocking or else it would make them soft and mushy, spoiling the recipe.
2. Now gently rub mushrooms with olive oil and line them on a baking tray, setting your oven to 400.
3. In a wok, drizzle some olive oil and toss in all the vegetable along with beef. Cook till the vegetables are done and meat is tender.
4. Toss this cooked mixture along with egg and coconut flour into your food processor to get even   tiny chunks of vegetables. Do not overdo, because we don't want a paste.

5. Now heap spoonfuls of this mixture on mushroom caps laid on the tray and let it bake for 20 minutes or till it is brown and the mushrooms look cooked.
6. Serve hot with crispy lettuce or cabbage leaves, sprinkled with lemon juice and seasoned with rock salt and pepper.

Pork With Spicy Barbeque Sauce

Ingredients:

- 2 tablespoons roasted cumin powder
- 1 tablespoons dried oregano
- 1 teaspoon white pepper powder
- 2 teaspoons cayenne pepper
- Barbeque sauce for coating the meat and a bit of gravy
- 4 pounds of grass-fed pork with bone (the shoulder part would be more preferable)
- 4 teaspoons red chili flakes
- 2 tablespoons sea salt
- 2 tablespoons black pepper powder

Directions:

1. Take all the spices and put them together in a bowl and give them a nice mix.
2. Then take the meat and rub this spice mix all over with your hands digging into each corner and curve.
3. Wrap the meat tightly in a cling wrap and refrigerate. For best results have ample time in hand and leave it in the fridge over night. It could stay in the fridge for about three days.
4. After taking it out, take the cling film out and put in the slow cooker with half a cup and forget it for 8 to 10 hours. I suggest using a Crockpot for it as it saves you from having to check the meat again and again.
5. Once this step is over and done with your pork it would also be just as tender and can be pulled off from the bones with a fork.
6. Break the meat into juicy shreds and coat them with barbeque sauce which has all

flavors you need. Have some sauce extra for the gravy.

7. This meat-sauce mixture again goes back into the Crockpot for about an hour or so, before it is ready to be polished off the plate.
8. It takes approximately 12 hours to prepare excluding the marinating and serves about 4 to 6 people.

Mushroom And Meatballs In Homemade Tomato Sauce

Ingredients:

- ½ cup parsley
- Yolks of two eggs
- Sea salt to taste
- Freshly crushed black pepper
- 1-2 tablespoon grass-fed butter or ghee for frying meatballs
- 1 pound finely chopped mushrooms
- 1 pound grass-fed minced beef
- 5 to 6 crushed cloves of garlic

For the sauce you would need

- Approximately 2 pounds of fresh cherry tomatoes or any other tomatoes of your choice
- 2 ½ teaspoon of extra virgin olive oil
- Sea salt and pepper as per taste

Directions:
1. In a big mixing bowl take all Ingredients: for meatballs and mix them thoroughly.
2. Shape the mixture into balls slightly larger than how you want them.
3. Fry the balls in butter or ghee. This seals in flavors of all the aromatic herbs and garlic used.
4. For the sauce, add blanched and roughly chopped tomatoes to olive oil. You could also add some more garlic if you like the flavor.
5. Add salt and pepper and slow cook the sauce.
6. Let the sauce simmer and once it looks almost done add the meatballs.

7. Meatballs will release all the flavors while they absorb the delicious tanginess of the tomatoes.
8. This would take 20-25 minutes for the balls to get tender and succulent.

Pulled Pork With Brussels Sprouts

Ingredients:

- 1 tablespoon dried oregano

- 1 ½ teaspoons ground turmeric

- ¼ cup apple cider vinegar (optional)

- ¼ cup xylitol (optional)

- 2 pounds pastured pork shoulder

- 3 strips uncooked bacon

- Sea salt to taste

For Brussels sprouts:

- 1 teaspoon sea salt

- 1 tablespoon grass fed unsalted butter

- ½ pound Brussels sprouts, halved

- 1 teaspoon ground turmeric

Directions:

1. Mix together in a bowl salt, oregano and turmeric and rub it over the pork.
2. Place pork in a pot or a Dutch oven.
3. Place pork strips over it. Pour a little water over it.
4. Cover and cook for an hour until done.
5. Remove pork pieces. When cool enough to handle, shred the pork using a pair of forks.
6. Add it back to the pot. Add rest of the Ingredients:.
7. Heat thoroughly.
8. To make Brussels sprouts: Place all the Ingredients: of the Brussels sprouts on a baking sheet and toss well.
9. Bake in a preheated oven at 300 F for about 45 minutes until crisp.

Broccoli Soup

Ingredients:

- ¼ cup grass fed, unsalted butter
- 1 medium onion, chopped
- 6 cloves garlic, minced
- 1 teaspoon black pepper
- Himalayan pink salt to taste
- 1 large head broccoli
- 6 cups organic vegetable broth
- 1 ½ cups carrot, peeled, shredded
- 1 tablespoon fresh parsley, chopped

Directions:

1. Place a large, heavy saucepan with butter over medium heat.

2. Add garlic and onion and sauté until fragrant.
3. Add carrot and stock and stir. Cover and bring to a boil.
4. Add broccoli, cover, and boil.
5. Reduce heat and simmer for a while.
6. Uncover and simmer for another 10 minutes. Remove from heat.
7. Blend with an immersion blender until smooth.
8. Ladle soup in individual soup bowls. Garnish with parsley and serve.

Hanger Steak With Herb Butter

Ingredients:

- 1 tablespoon lemon juice

- 6 cups spinach

- 3 tablespoon MCT or Bulletproof Brain Octane oil or coconut oil

- 8 tablespoons grass fed unsalted butter at room temperature

- Sea salt to taste

- 2 hanger steak (½ pound each)

- 2 lemons, grate the rind, chop the remaining part into wedges

- 4 tablespoons fresh herbs like oregano, rosemary or thyme

- 2 tablespoons chives, minced

Directions:

1. Apply oil over the steak and rub it well. Set aside for a while.
2. Mix together rest of the Ingredients: except spinach in a bowl and set aside.
3. Sprinkle salt over the steak and place on a preheated grill (medium high heat) and grill for a couple minutes.
4. Lower the heat of the grill to medium low and grill for around 4 minutes each side for rare or 5-6 minutes for medium rare.
5. Place the steak on a plate. Spoon about 2 ½ to 3 tablespoons of the herbed butter over each steak. Set aside for a while.
6. Slice the steak across the grain.
7. Serve with spinach. Pour the cooked juice over it and serve.

Berry Bowl

Ingredients:

- 1 cup fresh blueberries, rinsed
- 1 cup fresh strawberries, rinsed
- ½ cup fresh basil, rinsed
- 1 cup fresh raspberries, rinsed
- Juice of a lemon

Directions:

1. Remove the stem of the strawberries and discard it. Chop the strawberries into small pieces.
2. Mince the fresh basil.
3. Add blueberries, strawberries, raspberries and most of the basil to a bowl.
4. Toss well.
5. Pour lemon juice all over and toss again.

6. Divide into 4 dessert bowls. Refrigerate for a while if desired.
7. Sprinkle remaining basil on top and serve.

Cakes

Ingredients:

- 6 tablespoons unsalted grass fed butter at room temperature

- 1 teaspoon vanilla extract

- ½ teaspoon cocoa powder

- A small pinch pink Himalayan salt

- 3 pastured eggs at room temperature, separated

- 6 ounces 85% dark chocolate, chopped

- 6 tablespoons xylitol or 3 tablespoons xylitol and 3 tablespoons erythritol, powdered

- ½ tablespoon sweet rice flour (If it is not available, then do not use it)

Directions:
1. Line 9 muffin cups with paper liners and set aside.
2. Melt the chocolate in a double boiler until smooth.
3. Add half the sweetener, salt, and yolks to a bowl and beat with an electric mixer for around 3 minutes until thick and lighter in color.

4. Add this into the bowl of melted chocolate and fold gently. Add vanilla, cocoa and sweet rice flour and fold.
5. Add whites to a bowl and beat until soft peaks are formed. Add remaining sweetener and beat until stiff peaks are formed.
6. Add this to the chocolate batter and fold again.
7. Using a spoon, fill the muffin cups with the batter. Fill up to ¾ the cup.
8. Bake in a preheated oven at 350 F for around 20-22 minutes.

Bulletproof Liver Sausage

Ingredients:

- ¼ tsp. of onion powder
- ¼ tsp. of ground or rubbed Sage
- ¼ tbsp. of Xylitol
- 1/8 tsp. of Ginger
- ¼ tsp. of Marjoram
- 2 lbs. of grass-fed beef liver
- ½ tsp. of sea Salt
- ¼ tsp. of Ground White-Pepper (cayenne)
- ¼ tsp. of Nutmeg

Directions:

1. Steam the liver until it's barely cooked.

2. Place all the Ingredients: in the container of food processor and process.
3. This spreadable liver sausage (also known as liverwurst) can usually be eaten as it is or it can be served on open-faced sandwiches or crackers.

Delicious Meatballs

Ingredients:

- 4 tsp. of Fish Sauce
- 2 tsp. of Sesame Oil
- 4 tsp. of Coconut Oil
- 4 tbsp. of Coconut, shredded
- 1 lb. of Grass-Fed Beef
- 4 Green Onions, thinly sliced
- Sea salt (to taste)

Directions:
1. Preheat the oven at 350 F.
2. Mix all the Ingredients:, except for the oil, together in a mixing bowl.
3. Mix the Ingredients: together and shape the meatballs.

4. Heat the coconut oil in the skillet and cook the meatballs until brown.
5. Line a baking tray with foil and bake in the oven at 350 F for around 25 minutes. Then serve.

Crockpot Pork

Ingredients:

- 2 tbsp. of Ground Cumin
- 1 tbsp. of White Pepper, ground
- 1 tbsp. of Black Pepper, ground
- 2 tsp. of Cayenne Pepper
- 1 tbsp. of Dry Oregano
- 4 lb. of Bone in Pork Shoulder
- 3 tbsp. of Smoked Paprika
- 2 tbsp. of Chili Powder
- 2 tbsp. of Sea Salt
- BBQ-Sauce

Directions:

1. Aside from the BBQ-Sauce and pork shoulder, combine all the Ingredients: in a bowl and mix well to make the spice-rub.
2. Rub the spice-rub all over the pork.
3. Tightly wrap the spice covered pork in a plastic wrap; refrigerate it for a minimum of 3 hours or up to 3 days.
4. Unwrap the meat; put it in crock pot, add ¼ cup of filtered water; and place crock pot on a low heat and cook the meat for about 8-10 hours till it becomes fork-tender.
5. Transfer the meat to a cutting board. Empty the remaining liquid from the crockpot.
6. Pull the pork apart by tearing it into shreds using two forks.
7. Place the shredded pork back into the crockpot and cover it with BBQ Sauce
8. Continue to cook on a low heat for a further 30- 60 minutes till hot. Then serve and enjoy.

Pork Chops With Herb Crust And Wilted Dandelion Greens

Ingredients:

- 2 teaspoons Brain Octane C8 MCT Oil

- 1 ½ tablespoon grass-fed butter

- 1 bunch dandelion greens, trimmed, washed and roughly chopped

- Sea salt

- 1 tablespoon each minced fresh parsley, oregano, sage, and thyme

- 2 bone-in pork chops, room temperature

Directions:

1. In a small bowl, combine herbs and 1 teaspoon sea salt. Coat both sides of the pork chops with the herb/salt mixture.

2. Heat a heavy pan over medium heat. Add the Brain Octane C8 MCT Oil and the chops. Cook until the chops are golden, four to five minutes each side.
3. Remove the pan from the heat and add the butter, tossing the chops to coat. Plate the chops and put them aside.
4. Put the pan back on the heat and add dandelion greens, cooking in butter and drippings without turning, for two minutes.
5. Top the pork chops with the dandelion greens, drizzle with pan drippings and serve.

Tres Leches Cake

Ingredients:

Cake

- ½ cup monk fruit (brown)
- 6 eggs
- 1 tsp vanilla powder (or 1 tbsp vanilla extract)
- 2 tsp baking soda
- 2½ cups blanched almond flour
- ¾ cup unsalted butter (or Bulletproof Grass-Fed Ghee)
- ½ cup coconut flour
- ½ cup coconut milk
- 1 tbsp lemon juice

Tres leches 27 oz coconut cream

- 2-3 tbsp monk fruit

- 1 scoop Bulletproof Vanilla Bean Energy Collagen Protein

- 1 tsp vanilla extract

Coconut whipped cream

- 27 oz coconut cream

- 1-2 tbsp monk fruit

- 1 scoop bulletproof french vanilla creamer

Directions:
1. Preheat oven to 350ºF.
2. Mix all the cake ingredients together in a large bowl using a hand mixer.
3. Pour into an 8x8 greased, parchment-lined dish or a rectangle/slice tin.
4. Bake for 30 minutes or until cooked through and golden.

5. Meanwhile, make the tres leches by adding condensed milk, vanilla and sweetener into a medium-sized saucepan and bring the mix to a soft boil. Reduce for 30 minutes or until it's reduced by half and has thickened. Stir occasionally, especially toward the end to prevent the mixture from burning on the bottom.
6. Once the cake is finished baking, allow it cool.
7. Once the homemade condensed coconut milk is ready and off the heat, add Vanilla Bean Energy Collagen Protein and whisk until combined.
8. Poke the top of the cake to make a lot of holes and pour the condensed coconut milk mixture over the top so the cake absorbs all that tasty goodness.
9. Place cake in the refrigerator to set. Place a heavy mixing bowl (or the bowl from your

stand mixer) in the freezer to chill for the coconut whipped cream.

10. Add the solid coconut cream to the chilled mixing bowl and use a hand mixer or stand mixer to whip it. Add sweetener of choice and French Vanilla Creamer and continue whipping until the cream stiffens.

11. Spread the coconut whipped cream evenly over the cake and top with fresh berries. Once you dig into a slice of this keto tres leches cake, you may never go back to the traditional version.

Spinach Empanadas

Ingredients:

Crust:

- 1 tablespoon Lakanto classic sweetener

- ½ teaspoon fine sea salt

- 6 tablespoons (90 grams) refrigerated ghee, cut into pieces

- 1 large egg, organic, pasture raised, cold

- 1 ½ cups (158 grams) almond flour

- ½ cup tapioca flour aka: tapioca starch

Egg wash:

- 1 pinch salt

- 1 pinch Monk Fruit sweetener

- Mix everything well with a whisk or hand blender to integrate. (You can do this step up to 1 day before and keep refrigerated.)

- 1 pasture raised organic egg

- 1 pasture raised organic egg yolk

Directions:

Empanada pastry

1. Combine the almond flour, tapioca flour, sweetener, salt and ghee in a meals processor, or use a pastry blender in a bowl. Pulse or blend till the texture of coarse meal.
2. In a small bowl, whisk the egg and then add to the dry Ingredients:. Pulse/blend again till dough comes together. If you`re mixing in a bowl, you might also additionally want to use your fingers to carry the dough collectively at the end.
3. Form dough into a rectangle. Wrap in plastic wrap. Refrigerate for at least 1 hour.

4. When you`re ready to bake, preheat oven to 360 °F.
5. Remove pastry from fridge bring to room temp: roll out one round of dough in between sheets of parchment; cut with the largest cookie cutter.
6. Carefully lay circles (ideally must be cold) onto a perforated tray with a Silpat mat or parchment paper. Varnish edges with egg wash. Add 1 tsp of Kite Hill cream cheese and some spinach filling on top, near the empanada as if you are folding the circle to form a "quesadilla" glaze with egg wash and bake until golden.
7. If the dough breaks, that`s okay! Just press it back into area and repair any holes/cracks that may have formed.

Avocado Stuffed With Garlic Prawns

Ingredients:

- ¼ cup grass fed butter
- 1 clove garlic, minced
- Juice of half a lemon
- ¼ cup parsley, chopped
- 2 large avocados, stoned
- ½ cup wild caught tiger prawns, raw
- Salt and pepper to taste

Directions:
1. Bring a small saucepan to a medium heat. Add the butter.
2. When the butter is melted add the garlic and prawns. Mix well.

3. Cook for around 3 minutes or until prawns are cooked.
4. Stir in the parsley, lemon and salt & pepper.
5. Fill the avocado with the prawn mixture, enjoy!

Spaghetti Squash With Sage Butter And Hazelnuts

Ingredients:

- 10 sage leaves
- ¼ cup hazelnuts
- Sea salt to taste
- 2 small spaghetti squash
- ½ cup grass fed butter
- Juice of half a lemon

Directions:
1. Take the flesh out of the squash and place on two separate plates.
2. Heat a large fry pan to a medium heat.
3. Add the butter and wait until it starts to foam.

4. Add the sage leaves and let them slightly crisp.
5. Add the hazelnuts, lemon juice and sea salt.
6. Spoon the sauce over the squash and enjoy!

Sockeye Salmon Pate

Ingredients:

- 1 pound of sockeye salmon, skinned
- ¼ cup fresh chives
- 1 cup grass fed cream
- Zest and juice of 2 lemons
- Salt and pepper to taste

Directions:

1. Simply combine all the Ingredients: together in a food processor and blend until smooth.

www.ingramcontent.com/pod-product-compliance
Lightning Source LLC
LaVergne TN
LVHW010220070526
838199LV00062B/4676